# UNlearning UNworthiness:

## The Journey to Becoming Intentional About Self-Love and Personal Development

LOREA M. SAMPLE

ISBN: 9780692821244

LCCN: 2016920774

Author: Lorea M. Sample

Foreword: Varian C. Brandon

Afterword: Tierra Destiny Reid

Editor: Tamika L. Sims, Ink Pen Diva, LLC

Book Cover Design: Christopher Davis, Jr., Ascension Marketing Company

Publisher: LMS Unlimited, LLC

LoreaSample.com

Columbia, SC 29203

bookings@loreasample.com

# DEDICATION

In loving memory of my grandmother, Virginia McCrea Cooper, who showed me how to love like God and how to be a lady and my father, Glenn Elliot Sample, who taught me to give life my absolute best and to never give up and to all of the Outcasts who deserve to know just how loved and awesome they are to me.

# CONTENTS

# ACKNOWLEDGMENTS

*Thank you to the following individuals who without their contributions this book would not be possible.*

I would like to thank my eternal best friends; God the Father, God the Son (Jesus) and God the Holy Spirit, without your constant presence in my life this book would not be possible.

I also must thank my supporter, encourager and loving mother, Loretta Lorea Sample, I love you forever and a day for being who you are and teaching me to do the same through your beauty, intelligence and resilience.....plus, you're just a really cool person!

Finally, to all of my family, church family and friends who have been there for me in your own special way, my heart swells with love and gratitude! Thank you and I love you all!

# FOREWORD

It was late fall in Atlanta and I was attending a leadership summit. As I walked in, I noticed this striking ebony beauty from across the room. She was engaged in conversation, not necessarily connected to what was going on around her, but there was an unmistakable acknowledgement in the atmosphere that she was there.

Yes, Lorea had arrived.

Not in the way that most might assume, considering she is a licensed minister, successful engineer and thriving entrepreneur. Yes, it was plain to see that she carried with her all the accoutrements of societal success, but still, there was something much deeper.

It was clear that Lorea had ARRIVED.

She had arrived at a place within herself that wasn't secured by her education or her expertise, but secured by a sacred surrender and a Divine understanding of who she is, whose she is and why she is.

I later learned that Lorea would be one of the speakers and when her time came to speak, I was most engaged and struck by her willingness to be in the moment and share with us how the very essence of her message had been challenged earlier in the room. Not challenged by a person, but by the question of "enoughness" she was oh so familiar with. It was the very question she had contended with for much of her life, the question she had found a way to overcome and the question she realized she was created and compelled to dismantle for others.

See one of the earlier speakers seemed as if she had already said everything Lorea had intended to say and Lorea began to play tug of war with the consideration that maybe what she had to say was no longer necessary. Well once she took her place on the stage, she, and all of us in attendance, knew that could not be further from the truth.

She was extraordinary!

It became clear why it happened the way it did.  It allowed Lorea to take us on a very present journey, in a step- by- step way of what it means to contend with and overcome feelings of unworthiness.

And she takes you on a very similar journey in her soul stirring book ......*Unlearning Unworthiness*.

Lorea shares very personal stories from her life and the wisdom and insight she gathered that allowed her to change her questions of worthiness into statements of value. You will be challenged, enlightened and empowered as she helps you to discover who you are, expand who you are and re-write the narrative regarding who you thought you always needed to be. Your journey through awareness and acceptance will strengthen your faith in your Creator and expand your faith in who you have been created to be and all you have been created to do.

Lorea is not just a teacher of her work, she is also a student, which is one of the reasons this book is so powerful.

Lorea's message of unlearning unworthiness is an important one. And it is extremely honorable to me that someone with such success would be willing to pull back the curtain on an issue that far too many successful women struggle with every day...in silence. For all intents and purposes, there wouldn't ever be a reason to think that such a powerful and successful woman could deal with feelings of unworthiness. To me, the value is not just in what she has written, but in the fact that she chose to write it.

She chose vulnerability and transparency over image and perception management, to be of service to other high achieving women leaders who share this story.

This book is an offering to those high powered women leaders who need to be reminded that their true value is high above rubies, that they are fearfully and wonderfully made and that unworthiness is not their portion. It's to the women who have the capacity to believe that unworthiness is a learned deception...and that it can be unlearned.

Varian C. Brandon
Master Coach & Leadership Mentor
Author of the *9 Indisputable Laws of Personal Power* (release 2017)

# INTRODUCTION

**Dear Reader,**

I never wanted to be that girl. The girl who dressed modestly, yet trendy, a high achiever, intelligent, makeup looking good, hair envied, banging career, blossoming entrepreneur, loves God and all around have it together, at least on the outside. A hypocrite. I never wanted to be a hypocrite, but I was and certainly not on purpose. I was convinced I was being genuine in my achievements, but I was *living* through them. I believed that earning a mechanical engineering degree, buying a house, and becoming an entrepreneur were the things that validated me and established my worth. The more I achieved, the better I was put together, the more money I made, the more I believed it was all just a result of being who I was.

This is how it all starts, and continues, the quest to fill a void and heal a wound created by struggling with unworthiness. It is a quest that is faithful in leaving you empty in the end. It was my place of self-imposed torment, isolation and shame. Although I was surrounded by people who loved and appreciated me, I was lonely. One day in April 2011, I woke up and decided I no longer wanted to be there anymore. The first question I asked myself was, *"How did I get here?"* I needed answers and I was desperate for a solution to the challenges and failed lessons perpetuated throughout my life. The buck had to stop with me.

I knew I was not alone. I began to observe the lives of women I knew and saw a great deal of the same signs and symptoms of a soul sickness that even the best intentioned life can acquire. A healing process took place in my life. I began to experience and see life through a healthy lens. I desired to stop doing and transform into being. I believed I could take control of the domain of my life by getting still, studying my life courses, and do my homework. I shifted the perspective of the lessons from my life's "teachers" to pass a course I had spent my life repeating. God and I began an ongoing conversation which put me on the path of UNlearning UNworthiness™ and I want to share it with you.

It is my hope that as I share this gift of liberation with you through this book, you will develop your process of unlearning specific mindsets, behaviors and patterns that leads you to the knowledge of your true worth. With expectation, create the space to develop the confidence and courage to not care about the opinions of others, the ability to create healthy boundaries for intentional living and the joy of embracing your Divine difference. I am excited for you! Welcome to the journey of UNlearning UNworthiness!

# CHAPTER ONE
## SPLITTING THE DIFFERENCE

*"You are God's idea and He knows how to express Himself."* –
Bishop Monroe Saunders

There are two sides that come with being different. We all want to be different, but with the benefits of being the same. We all want to stand out and be the difference maker, but without dealing with the spotlight of criticism that comes with it. Everyone loves a purple cow until they are aware that all the others are black and white. You are different. Conformity is so deceptive. Conformity to societal norms relieves us of any possible friction or push back. It allows your life, choices and habits to remain. It doesn't ruffle any feathers. It allows everyone around you to be comfortable with the thought and idea of you, but not the *reality* of you. The thought of you is what most people are comfortable with, even you. Your thoughts can change at any time to suit how we want to see things and how we want to feel. What you think about another person is not necessarily the reality of who they are unless they are being their authentic self. The reality of you is everything that comes with who you are, how you see things, how you do things, your gifts and talents. These things may evolve, but the essence of who you are never changes. These are the things that make up your *difference*. It is what you have that others do not. Your *difference* is what makes it impossible for you to blend in and conform even when you consciously and intentionally work at it.

How does attempting to conform your *difference* operate in the area of unworthiness? How does it show up in your life? Attempting to conform at the expense of your *difference* is what I like to call,

"*Splitting your difference.*" Splitting your difference is when you compromise who you are and concede your Divine identity for the comfort of others. Some splits are for friends. Some splits are for family. Some splits are for politics. Splitting can be manifested in multiple areas of your life, but the more it is done, the more there is a taking away of you. This is a taught and learned behavior that can put someone so deep into a cave of fear that if they even thing about emerging out of it, it causes them to go into the cave deeper. We are taught this behavior by those closest to us and at a young age. It is usually taught to us by our parents. When we are young, our thinking is molded with the least resistance. Our parents love us so much that they do not want to see us hurt in any way. They teach us what they know so we will be safe and protected. This teaching is either by instruction or by demonstration. Either way, it can leave us with the impression that we must cover up whom we are to be safe. We are taught to conform for survival. Not feeling and believing that your existence and the core of who you are (your *difference*) is worth recognition and acceptance is one of the toughest, rock bottom places to be in. Who else can you effortlessly be, but you?

The state of unworthiness can show up in various ways. The way we exist, express ourselves, and demonstrate our presence comes with a sound and melody. There are systems, structures, powers and people who do not like the sound of you. They attempt to silence you through the media, legislation, unrealistic standards of beauty, and educational institutions through *systematic mutation*. It is a systematic silencing in order to reduce or deaden the intensity of your voice/sound by the addition of another (voice/sound). *Whenever you Risk Expression*™ as Akilah Richards, one of my favorite writers, has coined, something at a cellular level happens. It stirs vibrations within and without and people begin to pick up on it. Not just any group of people, but your tribe. Your tribe is the people who get you. Although there are things you will have in common, there are still no two of you exactly the same. *Difference* is welcomed and much needed in your tribe.

Your difference is what validates your worth and need in the world. Accidental people do not exist. We are all a part of an intentional creation, with an intentional plan, for an intentional purpose. When we become consumed in the taking away of ourselves, *splitting our difference*, the people who need to hear our sound are unable to move. It is like a train carrying precious cargo. If the prime mover (the engine) is disconnected from the rest of the train, when the whistle blows (the sound) the rest of the train is left behind and is immobile. How much precious cargo (you) have you left immobile because of systematic mutation and splitting your difference?

Your Divine difference is your birthright. By birth, you are entitled to the rights and privileges that come with being you because God created you. It is exciting, but there is a disclaimer. You only obtain those rights and privileges by being you, not someone else. There is a flow that comes with being you. There is no need to force your natural existence. Once you are here, you are here. However, you do have to force what does not exist: your made up image of you. It is like trying to put a square peg into the round hole. No matter what you do to force it in, it will not fit. Even if you shave off the edges of the square peg and smooth it out to make it round, you have automatically taken away (split the difference) its original form and purpose. In doing this, we fail to consider the square space that the square peg was created to occupy. A void now exists there.

Being who you were created to be is liberating. You have the security of knowing that being authentically you is always right! It does not mean you are perfect or always know what to do in that knowledge, but it allows you to flow with the current of your life. As I mentioned before, everyone has a flow that comes natural to being them. Everyone has a flow given by God. When we surrender to our process of purpose we serve as an extension of God's love to others. He is the ocean, the source of our flow, and when we choose to live and serve in a great way we are like little rivers that bring forth water to the dry places in other's lives as well as our own. What an honor! What a choice!

Flowing, as well as struggle, is a choice. To choose struggle is to become the obstruction to our own flow. Flowing in our natural, but Divine creation and purpose, allows God to carve out the path of our flow. What is the path that God is carving out when we choose to flow? Our process. The path (the process) of our flow (difference) carved out by God will always lead us to our purpose. When we change, split, and/or disregard our difference in the world, we forfeit the created path to our purpose. This is what we all want. This is what we are all reaching for and looking to discover, knowledge of why we are here.

Unworthiness is the cancer that eats away from the beautiful perspective of what makes us unique. It eats away at the reality that our voice of hope needs to be heard by the hopeless. Or, that a simple smile can cause someone to reconsider doing life just one more time.

**Internalizing Difference as a Gift Empowers You to Be and Do**

To choose to flow is to reject flow obstruction and struggle. When we choose God's design for our path through internalizing our Divine difference we choose to adopt and incorporate His perspective and Divine motives. Through unlearning what we have known, we create the opportunity to learn something new. We cultivate our gift of choice or free will. We choose to learn the truth of who we are, and it is a beautiful truth. We begin to learn this beautiful truth through socialization and most importantly, identification. We begin to adopt and incorporate the Divine vision for ourselves that God intended from conception. We begin to identify with who we are at our core. When we discover what our unique qualities are, it is as though we have discovered buried treasure! We know without a shadow of a doubt that it is this Divine difference that makes us an original. We stand out instead of blending in with the crowd. We must be open to see our difference as a gift to appreciate and treat it with care. The human condition does not always encourage us to do that. Let us explore why we reject the things everyone loves about us, but we undervalue.

Have you ever had someone say to you, *"You are so good at that!"* or *"You are a natural!"* and you left the conversation not truly gripping what the big deal was because after all, everyone knows how to do what you do, right? Wrong. Skills and activities that you are naturally good at, even though you may work at it, do not come naturally to everyone else. We tend to think that the things that come naturally to us are not our gifts because they are so natural and so instinctual to who we are and what we do.

Our common view of what a gift is can jade our view of how precious our gifts and Divine difference are. We should honor and nurture them. Imagine your excitement as a child on your birthday. The time had come for you to open your gifts and discover the new and exciting toys or gadgets your parents or family members had given you. You were so excited at times, you almost exploded! The discovery process was the most stimulating part of opening the gifts because depending on what you discovered, you were going to either be a very happy camper or severely disappointed. You frantically ripped the wrapping paper off of the box, struggled to break the masking tape to open the box, and pull out the tissue paper. You are finally at the mountain top of your discovery experience; discovering the gift you are receiving. There it is finally, the gift.

For starters, let us go with the happy response: You are happy beyond words, jumping up and down with a smile a mile wide and are endlessly thankful for the gift and to the gift giver. On the other end of the spectrum, if you do not like the gift, there is no amount of acting classes that could prepare your facial expressions to be warm, welcoming and/or grateful at least for the thought of giving you a gift. Matter of fact, you wished that they did not even think. You do not like it and everyone knows it.

When it comes to our gifts from God we can use the example above to give us a view of ourselves we may not have considered:

1. Even though we can make a request as to the type of gift(s) we may want, He will give us the gift(s) suitable for us and His purpose. (1 Corinthians 12:11)
2. Like all gifts, they are freely given. There's nothing we can do to earn a gift.
3. We must be thankful for the gifts given to us by God. Gifts we are endowed with to lead and pursue our purpose.
4. We must recognize that even though we may not hold a particular gift in high regard, it is important to nurture it because God gives us gifts with intention.
5. We must learn to see the purpose of our gifts as an opportunity to share them and make a difference in the lives of others.

Our gifts empower us to be who we were created to be naturally, while clearing the path for us to do what we are called to do. This is the intent of our gifts. Earlier I mentioned the taglines of one of my favorite writers, Akilah Richards. If you are not familiar with her, she is from the island of Jamaica who has built a cool living with her husband as entrepreneurs. They are both known to be what they term as "location independent, digital nomads" and the parents of two intelligent, curious daughters who are unschooled world learners. One of Akilah's more prominent gifts is storytelling. Every time I read something she has written I feel like we are in a sista circle getting ready to change and take over the world.

She is also one of the reasons why I love being unapologetically black and a black woman who wears her hair big and lusciously natural. Although she continuously cultivates her storytelling skills and coachers others to do the same, it is naturally who she is as a person. Having worked with her, listened to some podcasts/audios, and read several of her writings, I can sincerely say that she embodies her gift. Her work is a direct reflection of who she is. She is a storyteller. We come into conflict with who we are when we first *do,* before we embrace our difference and first *be.* Most people skip the step of *being* and go straight to *doing* simply because we are not clear on what *being* is and how to do it.

To *be* is to be who you have been called to be, to live in that space, and occupy that place. Simply put, it is just who you are. There is no trying or force-fitting. There is no despising your make-up. You fully embrace everything that comes with being you. You are unapologetic about not judging your understaffing, but instead focusing on that beautiful thing called your difference. It is being unbothered by the fact that even though there are other people with the same gift(s) as you, you know you have been touched by Heaven to use yours uniquely. It is pure confidence. This is the type of confidence that only comes from experience and a place of being. When we put the cart before the horse and *do* before being, we can lack confidence and approach our life assignments from a place of fear instead of courage. The world can smell fear like sharks smell blood in the water. You will be perceived as a fraud when in reality, you only moved out of order. Everything has an order to it. What we give our focus and attention to first receives the most energy and power. Being then doing assists in putting your life in order.

## How to Capture Your Difference to Make a Difference

When I was in my twenties, I felt as if I was all over the place. In 2001, I received my Bachelor of Science Degree in Mechanical Engineering. This was around the same time of the September 11th Attacks and because of this, there was a widespread hiring freeze. I was unemployed. I did not care much about not having secured a job in my field of study because I was not fully convinced I wanted to be an engineer. I did not think it was for me. I was overqualified for everything I applied for at one of the popular malls in Columbia, SC, but a nice manager at Eddie Bauer named Nelson decided to give me a shot as a sales associate. I could not stand seeing clothes in the wrong place and/or disheveled so I was the go-to-gal for creating order on the floor and in the stock room. However, I was not the go-to-gal for Sallie Mae and Company so I needed a new gig, fast.

I then became a sales representative for a company that sold residential and commercial water treatment systems. I was good at it, really good. I understood the science because of my engineering background and I was not stuck behind a desk all day. Did I mention that the money was really good? On average, I was earning $20,000 a month. Sallie Mae and Company was off of my back, I went on a company paid trip to Cancun, fully furnished my 2-bedroom apartment with cash, and was completely stressed out. I worked six days a week, traveled all six of those days and was down to a size six because of the stress that came with the job (an accidental perk), and had no life. Can someone say deuces, exit stage left?!

Here I was unemployed again with no plan and after a brief stint as a part-time waitress and customer service representative for a health insurance company I decided to go back to school and study for a licensed practical nursing degree. Why? Honestly, because I felt as if I could. I was able to secure a 2-year contract job as a student nurse technician at a local hospital working 3rd shift. This allowed me to go to school during the day and make a living at night. It was challenging, but I did it. At the end of the program, I knew without any doubt being a nurse was not for me so I returned to my home base, engineering.

After being out of the engineering industry for 3+ years, the first and only position that I applied and interviewed for hired me and I was relocated to North Myrtle Beach, SC where I worked for a startup company. I loved it! I lived at the beach, but never went to the beach. I traveled all across the country, saw different places and experienced the various dialects and cultures in America. I made a decent living and I was content. However, I could never find a home church there that compared to what I was receiving at my church home in Columbia, SC. I would travel, every weekend, 2.5 hours one way to be in church every Sunday. I never missed a Sunday. My spiritual growth was more important to me than my contentment at the beach, so I opted to relocate back to Columbia, SC, where I accepted an engineering position that paid a tad less, but was worth it because I was back at my base.

From start to end, the total time of that journey took a little over six years. That was over half of my twenties. I was scattered, worked hard, and learned hard all for me to return back to my base. When I eventually returned to engineering a good friend of mine said to me, *"You were an engineer trying to be a nurse!"* We laughed about it, but I did not miss one of the important lessons that I learned from that process. I was an engineer from the beginning, but I was not sold on it. I did not *feel* like an engineer, did not *act* like the stereotypical engineer, I did not *think* I was a genius like my college mates, but that is what made me different. I am analytical, but my personality and communication skills assist me more in my career than my intellect. I care about people, not projects. I spent over six years re-capturing my difference and once I did, I gained a new perspective on it. I no longer saw what made me different as an engineer as a weakness or a negative. I realized my difference was not a curse. I realized that some things were not going to change about me and those were the things I needed to seize and take possession of as a blessing and gift. I decided to use those things to become an influencer and difference maker.

You were not created to be the sum of the thoughts toward you. You were created to be in accordance to God's thoughts towards you. You were created intentionally and thoughtfully. You must willingly cooperate and agree with these thoughts. If you disagree with, are ignorant of, or disregard Heaven's original intent for your being here, you forfeit the plans and purpose for your life. Our thoughts can take us to some far and away places. Everything we think is not true or close to reality. Heavenly thoughts come our way to keep us focused on truth. These thoughts may not agree with how you think about yourself, but that is not a requirement for them to be true. We must condition our thoughts to be pure and Heavenly. We do not have to believe everything we think and we certainly do not have to go where they take us. We must develop our thinking to assist us in evolving into who we were created to be. When we have a negative thought enter into our mind we have one of two choices to make: 1. Accept it. 2. Reject it. When we choose to not counter the negative thought and allow ourselves to stay there thus meditating on it, we accept it. When we counter the negative thought with the truth of what God has said about us or a situation, we reject it (2 Corinthians 2:5). No matter what choice we make, that thought will manifest a reality in our lives directly connected to that thought. We must choose our thoughts wisely.

I tend to have some quirky perspectives on negative thoughts, so I ask you to please indulge me on this one. I believe the beauty about a negative thought is you have the opportunity to choose it or not. Free will is so delicious like that, don't you think? Just like struggle, your thoughts are chosen. We choose to think and we choose what we think. Thinking is not a visceral reaction or response that you do not have to think about. Thinking requires thinking. It is a conscious act that you do now in order to impact your future, even

24

if it is only five minutes from now. We can make the choice to think peaceably about ourselves and be at peace with who we are. This is not only therapeutic for you, but for others.

I believe that whether consciously or unconsciously, we are always living and working to get back to our base; our original way of being. God knew exactly what He was doing when He chose what kind of temperament you would have. He knew if paragraphs not being justified when typed would give you the heebie jeebies. He knew you would have the gift of gab that enables you to sell a dead goat to a billionaire. Stop the suffering within your soul. Start the process of untethering yourself from the idea of who you thought you were born to be and surrender to the reality of your divine difference. Surrender so you can see the Divine order of your life.

Making a difference in the lives of others is always a part of the plan for our lives. There is already a group of people attached to our life we are called to impact and influence. When we capture what makes us different, we understand that it is what God uses to accomplish His will and touch the lives of others. You begin to accept the responsibility of not hiding and co-creating the purposes of God through Divine difference. Some people will not be able to hear a message they need to hear except at your frequency. Others may not be able to feel the urgency of making a life-changing decision for the better without you providing the vibration. The lesson here is to care for and embrace your difference for the purpose of giving others permission to do the same. The intent of our hearts cannot be seen. It is through visible action that most will need to see it done. When they see the possibility, they can become the possibility.

## Your Difference is the Pathway to Your Purpose

When it comes to our gifts and talents, we can be easily swayed in our own mind that mere possession of them is our purpose. For example, if someone is a prodigy as a pianist, we would qualify and quantify their purpose around the gift to play the piano. It is quite natural for us to put so much emphasis on the gifting that we miss the significance of purpose and intent. What makes us unique is what draws others in to empower, educate and encourage, but it is not our purpose. It serves as a tool. Our gifts make room for us to fulfill the purpose of God through and in our lives. Many people live and die utilizing their gifts, but never realizing their purpose. Your difference is a mobilizer. It creates movement once you respond to your life's calling.

Being a regular, active church member for over 13 years, I experienced many people with the gift of a beautiful singing voice. Some voices have a calming effect, others are encouraging, and some are soul-stirring. Each one of those voices has ministered to me over the years, but each one, when used *purposely*, will lead others to their purpose if they follow God's leading. More often than not most stop at the calling and believe their purpose is singing. Perspective often can be lost or distorted when we stop short at the difference. We forfeit eternal destiny fulfillment for the gift. Do not misunderstand me, gifts are great and needed. Everyone has at least one of them, but most of us possess a few. It is the purposeful use of the gift that creates difference, which creates the pathway to purpose.

Developing your difference through identification, knowing who you are as a reflection of God in the earth, gives you a corrected lens view on your purpose. At our core, this is what we are all reaching for at the end of the day. Purpose in God is where you find your worth and significance of having a focused life. When you recognize, nurture, and internalize your difference, purpose becomes clear and it becomes our priority. Difference serves as a filter that clears the muddy waters of our life and positions us to shine our light in some unlikely and amazing places. We become clear. We become confident. We become conduits of Divine empowerment and love. Worthiness is then learned through the discovery and awareness that our lives truly are important and worth living.

### AFFIRMATION

I am intentional in my being.

I am impactful in my difference.

I am stretching the boundaries towards my eternal destiny.

I am created to create change

## UNlearning Exercises

1. List the top three complimentary attributes you are constantly told is your gift; your *difference*.

_____

_____

_____

2. What are your honest thoughts about your gifts?

_____

_____

_____

3. If they are negative thoughts, list some scriptures that reaffirm God's plans for your gifts.

_____

_____

_____

4. List ways your difference can purposely serve others.

_____

_____

_____

UNlearning UNworthiness

# CHAPTER TWO
## WORKING IT OUT, INSIDE

*"Internal honesty births honest expression."* – Lorea M. Sample

We all live in two worlds at the same time: the external and the internal. The external world is the easiest to live in on a daily basis. What everyone observes on the outside is what they believe to be true until they see something different. Yes, there are some that can discern whether it is the real you or not, but most people are not sensitive enough to make such a judgement. People will quickly judge who you are based off of what they see, which is not uncommon. God knew this about us. As the prophet Samuel was at the house of Jesse to anoint the next king of Israel, God noted that He does not look at a person's outward appearance as we do, but He looks at their heart (1 Samuel 16:7). The thoughts of our heart influence what we think and we perpetually have a conversation about it in our internal world.

The internal world, in my opinion, is harder to live in every day; the only person that resides there is you. It is a place where only you have access, unless you choose to give it to someone else. No one knows the commentary that you have with yourself about yourself day after day. When the thoughts are positive or favorable, your internal world can resemble Sesame Street. Your days are sunny and everything's A-OK. You feel good about yourself, you speak well of yourself and everyone knows it. The way you walk, the way you talk and how you dress all visually demonstrate how you feel about yourself on the inside.

However, there can be times when your internal world can look like a battle scene from the Civil War. It can be vicious, bloody and a lot of friendly fire exchanged. We have to live with ourselves, but are frustrated at the same time. When dealing with unworthiness, we can say some of the most abusive and damaging things to ourselves. We can become our own worst enemy. We believe we are being brutally honest with ourselves, but the truth is we are being self-destructive. We lack patience, mercy, grace, love and understanding as we process pain and disappointment. We deny ourselves of what we require others to have. By doing this, we demonstrate our belief that we are not worthy of receiving what we need to engage in healthy healing. Oh, the lies we tell ourselves when dealing with unworthiness! This fight we internally engage in can be won, but we must unconditionally let go.

## Letting Go of Struggle for Progress

One of the most powerful things you can do is let go. Letting go of anything is not easy. Even if what we are holding on to is toxic or infectious to our soul, it still can be challenging to open our hands and hearts to release it. The need to release things, people, thoughts, hurts and/or feelings always takes you to doors of choice. A vital part of how our life functions is through a continual series of choices. The better choice you make for your life, the better life is to you. The question is, how do you choose what is best for you? The first step is to know who you are. Who we are as individuals, I believe, can be made up of different flavors, facets and flaws. However, I also believe that at our core, at our purest self, we are relatively simple. What makes us tick individually is not complex; we just need to get through the miseducation of ourselves by unlearning our way to the truth of ourselves. This requires change.

Change comes with challenges. The types of challenges that we deal with depend on the part of ourselves that is being challenged. If we are being honest with ourselves, there are some parts of us that we will fight to keep. It does not matter whether it is a bad part or not, it is ours and we will rebel to keep it just the way it is even if it causes us to suffer. Why? Well, because it is ours! As women, we tend to give away so much of ourselves through relationships, careers and family that any piece we lay claim to is off the market. Or, because *"this is the way I've always been"* changing can feel like a betrayal of who we have known ourselves to be in life. Out of nowhere, it seems you realize you can choose differently, just for you.

Suffering is a choice and letting go of it for the sake of progress takes courage and faith. The "struggle for existence" becomes our default. According to Dictionary.com, struggle for existence is defined as:

> *- the competition in nature among organisms of a population to maintain themselves in a given environment and to survive to reproduce others of their kind.*

In laymen terms, you struggle for existence by fighting yourself and everyone like you to remain the same and affect those you have influence with to be like you. This process is very common with parent/child relationships. In the parent's effort to teach their child to be better than them, more successful in life than them, they unknowingly transfer fear or project their self-image. Our parents in the impressionable years of our lives are the teachers with the greatest impact on us. The impact can be positive or negative. Our parents have the ability to introduce, or sometimes force, ideas and beliefs on us for various reasons. They can teach out of fear, protection, love, control, manipulations, or hate. Once these ideas and beliefs are presented to us, we have one of two choices to make; accept or reject it. It is no surprise that most of the time we choose to accept it. We may not agree with the specific belief, but we accept it as part of our mindset because after all, why would our parents lie to us?

It is in my opinion that we are all born with the Divine breath of God on the inside. Because of that piece of God we possess, most, if not all of us, have a strong desire to have a relationship with a higher being. We have a sense that there is someone "out there" that is greater, stronger and wiser than ourselves; a higher being who can give us guidance. We seek this guidance from our parents until we are mature enough to go on the search for the truth of who is this greater being. Until then, our natural default is to apply those attributes mentioned previously to our parents.

When we are underexposed and inexperienced socially and in age, our parents are our spiritual and moral guides. They are like gods to us and serve as the first point of reference of our existence. It can seem disloyal to question or reject any part of the lessons our first teachers taught us, but that is actually a sign of maturity and growth. Once you begin to question a long-held mindset, you awaken the space within you for progress towards something new.

## Choosing to Heal Your Pain Is an Unselfish Act

I will admit it, going into the direction of something new and leaving behind what you have always known can be scary. It can scare you into emptying your bladder spontaneously without notice! Fear is a powerful energy and experience that can paralyze and hold you hostage to a lie. It takes courage to choose truth. This is why every step you take towards truth is a step made towards progress. What is progress? What does it look like for you? In the case of unlearning unworthiness, progress begins with making the choice to heal from your pain. When you feel worthless there is an injury that has taken place in your soul. Injury to the soul can be a hard place to heal because of where it is located. Just as a surgeon sometimes must perform exploratory surgery to pinpoint the cause that is producing the effect, we must do the same with the soul.

It is not always obvious where our soul's pain is located and what is causing it. This is an important part of making real progress. You must be intentional and effective in your approach to healing your true self and not a persona or representative. You are worth it! You must believe, trust and embrace that truth. You are worth it. You are worth the time it takes to heal. You are worth the energy it takes to heal. You are worth pouring out the old and destructive mindsets in order to heal. It is a conscious and loving act towards yourself for progress.

*Soul Excavation* is the term I like to use to describe this process. Although I have not coined this term, in my opinion, it is an accurate description of the approach we can take when healing an injury to the soul. One of my favorite subjects in grade school and life in general is history. I do not live in the past, but I love learning about it. History has always given me a better understanding of the present realities and a deeper appreciation and knowledge of how we have gotten "here." When I look at different television shows and documentaries about ancient times in the Middle East and Africa, there is usually a segment which focuses on an area in an archaeological site. The overall site is always clearly marked off and divided into smaller sections. You approach a soul excavation in the same way. For example, you may be in pain in the area of relationships; that is the overall site area. Then, there are different types of relationships such as family, romantic, spiritual, and friendships; these are the smaller divided sections. From there, you can choose one area to excavate and explore.

Excavation and exploration require the right tools. For soul excavation there are several tools to pull from such as:

- Focus
- Prayer
- Willingness to Confront
- Wisdom

- Self-Awareness
- Wise Counsel
- Commitment to Truth
- Stillness
- Honest Communication and
- Letting Go

From the list above, one of the most important tools to have in the beginning and throughout the process is the willingness to confront. This is what allows you to dig deep and reveal the treasures and truth of what has always been on the inside. The willingness to confront is the shovel that breaks the fallow ground of your heart. It clears the way to change. However, once the "digging" begins in a specified area, we must be careful and mindful with how we uncover and reveal places within ourselves that we have never fully dealt with before. We do not want to cause more damage to a wounded area with tools of negative destruction such as:

- Guilt
- Self-judgement
- Condemnation
- Negative Talk or
- Denial

Instead, we want to restore and preserve the area with tools of patience, love and grace. The metaphor of an archaeological excavation to describe how to heal parts of the soul may seem too much, but it is just that serious. If we are not careful we can make things worse during the process. You must protect the uncovered spaces by protecting your peace and energy at all costs. That takes work, focus and intention. You are worth the time it takes to be whole.

## Being Empowered By Choosing to Do Your Work

Let us have a moment of clarity, this is work. It takes time, energy, consistency and effort. You will resist it and at times it will not feel good. You will get frustrated with yourself. You will fight the urge to throw in the towel and quit. These are facts. As you find your way through the tears and dust of your past, you will begin to discover some things about yourself. It is exciting and surprising to receive an unexpected gift of empowerment. You begin to give yourself permission to unlearn what you always believed about yourself and learn how you are supposed to reflect God in the world around and within you.

Being empowered to learn something new, something that is truth to your experience, is like being given keys of authority to open multiple doors. You hold the keys to discovery, self-love, healing and purpose. You become empowered to intentionally choose you, do your work and understand there are some things within your control, including you. You can be empowered to control your thoughts about yourself because every thought you have is not true. You can control your internal environment as well. You are aware that you do not need to be entertained by every TV show that comes on, listen to every song on the radio, read every post, or embrace every opportunity. You are empowered to choose.

You have options to how you want to feel. You may be angry about something, but you get to choose how you channel this anger. You may not feel joyful on any given day, but you get to choose to flow through the day with the spirit of gratitude. You get to choose your way to change. Your desire to do you differently becomes a force that when coupled with progress, it becomes a part of your evolving identity. When we connect with God and build a relationship with Him, we connect to the source of our true identity. Through our unlearning process, we do not change who we are, but evolve into who we were created to be. Evolving requires you to get to know and grow into what is unfamiliar, but was always there.

The year 2013 was transformational year for me. That year, I was committed to change in every area of my life. One of the areas that piqued my interest out of the blue, seemingly, was makeup. I became a makeup junkie (still am) and YouTube was my pusher. I watched video after video of some of my favorite beauty vloggers to learn about eyebrow arching techniques, blemish coverage hacks, and the latest product features and tutorials. I was sold out! One day as I was perfecting my eyebrow arching technique, I looked at myself in the mirror, paused and began to admire my work. I then said out loud, *"I like this!"* Not as in the look of my makeup (even though it looked great), but *this* as in being a girly girl who loves playing in makeup. I realized in that moment I never knew that side of me existed, but it was always there. Up until that point in my life I taught myself that survival was more important than my self-esteem. "Who needs makeup?!" is what I would say until that day. I paused, looked in the mirror, and I saw me. It gave me the warm fuzzies!

Do I need makeup to survive? No, but I learned that I wanted makeup in my beauty regimen. It made me feel awesome. I was choosing what I wanted and what I wanted was me, not a rigid version of me. You experience freedom when you choose to be yourself. True freedom is choosing what you want to do and doing it. You begin living a life of liberty when you do what you want, not what you need, because you can. Unlearning what you once knew to be true about yourself and discovering what is true about you is freedom. You have the right to change your mind. With any new freedom, comes a new responsibility. My new freedom came with the responsibility to teach and empower other women to do the work of inner healing for holistic growth in their lives.

Unlearning Unworthiness was my Divine gift and life class given to me, to give to you. Doing your work of inner healing is the gift that keeps on giving. Your inner healing is necessary for the healing of others because it serves as a model for others.

We learn in different ways. Some of us are audio, some visual, and some are a combination of the two. If you are anything like me, you learn best through demonstration. Hearing and seeing information is great, but it is challenging for me to comprehend what I am being taught unless I apply the information I have received. That is when it all clicks for me. In general, that is how most people navigate through inner healing, by demonstration. Healing is in the doing, digging, crying, accepting, confronting, writing, forgiving, and changing. This dynamic is what makes it possible for progressive inner healing to become permanent. The coupling of practical actions and spiritual principles and truths leads you through healthy healing of your soul.

### **AFFIRMATION**

My work is for me to do.

I have confidence in God's process for my life.

I work for progress and am thankful for my new normal.

I am graced to complete my work.

## UNlearning Exercises

1. List the top three areas you need healing in:

   _____

   _____

   _____

2. What mindsets are hindering your progress and why?

   _____

   _____

   _____

3. What "new" thing(s) about yourself are you learning during this process?

   _____

   _____

   _____

4. What do you believe is your new responsibility in the new freedom you're walking in?

   _____

   _____

   _____

# CHAPTER THREE
## SHELVING

*"Take yourself off of the shelf. You are loved."* – Lorea M. Sample

As a child, we all had *that* toy that we had to have. It was usually during a special holiday like Christmas when retailers ramped up the marketing to children or for your birthday. Life was not worth living if you did not have *that* toy. Once you received it, like most kids, you played with it as if it was going out of style, initially. This phenomenon lasted for about a week, each year. After a week or so, you were now on to the next thing and the toy that you just had to have goes on the shelf. You would forbid anyone from giving it away or throwing it in the trash, even if it was broken. As long as you could see it, locate it, and retain possession of it, you were okay. The toy was no longer a priority, but you still counted it as a necessary part of your life. I call this process *shelving*.

There are parts of us that once were a priority. They are parts that we once loved and valued about ourselves. It was not necessary to tell us that we were precious and priceless because for most of us, there was a season when no one told us otherwise. Then it happened, the moment that we were taught we were not who we believed ourselves to be. That is when life as we knew it changed. As a result, we began the process of shelving.

## Shelving and the Lack Mentality

As a child, I was head-over-heels in love with musicals. *The Sound of Music*, *West Side Story*, and *Cats* were some of my favorites. What I loved about them so much was that they took me out of my reality and allowed me to be whoever and however I wanted to be. My childhood was a bit tough. There were times when there was no money, no heat in the middle of a Philadelphia winter, no food, and no lights/electricity. Life at times was "tight," which caused me to become "tight". The lack of the essentials around me began to teach me to have a lack mentality. On the inside, in my spirit, I knew there was the existence of abundance, but the lack that was around me was all that I saw; it was my reality. I followed suit with what I believed to be my reality, lack. Lack manifests in your life in different ways and one is as a lack mentality. A lack mentality can be creative in the way it chooses to show up, trust me I know. *Dictionary.com* defines lack as:

- Deficiency or absence of something needed, desirable, or customary.

Lack is not always monetary, although we tend to associate it with money. According to the definition, there are three basic categories that lack is taken into consideration:

1. The absence/deficiency of something needed.
2. The absence/deficiency of something desired.
3. The absence/deficiency of something customary.

Let us first deal with the lack of something needed. When we shelve ourselves of what we need, we are in a desperate position. When we become deficient or absent of the necessary parts of ourselves we begin to waste away in the form of self-sacrifice. It can feel like a slow death of the soul. Mentally, we convince ourselves that it is for the best for everyone involved. We tell ourselves that we do no need to get that 6-8 hours of sleep or that it is not necessary to spend some time with ourselves, alone. We tell ourselves self-care is a luxury, not a necessity. We teach ourselves that everyone else is priority over us. We begin to master shelving who we are which nurses a lack mentality.

What feeds that mentality further is the deficiency of what we desire in our lives. I am single and have never been married...yet! Over the course of a decade, I tried to convince myself that it was not a big deal if I did not marry. I have not checked this statistic, but I am confident that the mortality rate of single people who never marry is 0%. In other words, there is a 100% survival rate for those who remain single, I am pretty sure of it. This is what I would tell myself every time the desire to marry became evident, emotionally. One week I would pray for my husband to manifest, and the next week I would pray for God to take away the desire to marry. It was exhausting! Then one day, when I was back on my send-me-my-Boaz kick, God cut me off mid-sentence and asked me:

> God: What do you want?
> Me: Huh? I want to be married of course...that is what I am praying for.
> God: Yes, today you are, what about tomorrow? Or next month?
> Me: sigh...ok, I gotcha.

God tells us that a person who is double-minded is unstable in all of their ways (James 1:8). I did not think I was unstable in everything that I did, but I was according to the standard of God. God is always right, so choose progress over struggle. A lack mentality can influence you to shelve your desires. It will deceive you into believing that it is okay to not want what you desire. When faced with making a final decision about marriage, something unexpected happened. I discovered that it was challenging for me to come out and say what I wanted. It was just me and God, yet I felt so vulnerable and ashamed. It almost felt like "the money talk."

The average person does not like to talk about money. It is easier for people to talk about not having money than having money to do whatever you like, hence, a lack mentality. Not voicing what you desire for yourself is a direct result of a lack mentality and shelving.

When we shelve ourselves of what is customary, we take ourselves out of our Divine position. What is customary to a person is what is usual, normal, or out of habit. When we place parts of ourselves outside of where God intended us to be, what is abnormal begins to feel normal. What is wrong feels right. What is chaos, feels like peace. What is confusion looks like clarity. What is abuse feels like love. Unworthiness makes you believe that you do not deserve God's best for you. Unworthiness causes you to believe that receiving less and receiving last is ok. You were not designed to live life that way. By God's original design, we were created to live a life of abundance spiritually, relationally, physically, mentally, and emotionally. Abundance is not restricted to money or material things. Abundance is connected to wholeness. To be whole is customary. Every time we shelve ourselves from what is customary, Heaven petitions us by asking, "Will thou be made whole?"

Do you need all of who you are? Do you want to receive your Divine desires? Do you want what is customary from God through wholeness? Unlearning unworthiness enables you to choose to be abundantly you. Shelving parts of you from what is either necessary, desired or customary does not make them disappear. Those parts of you are always there, waiting for you to reclaim them.

Shelving, although not the most productive coping mechanism, has a bright side to it. When you put something on a shelf, it is still visible. You can still catch a glance of its beauty which can spark a memory of joy. As long as you have access to it, you still have hope. It is still within your reach and right to reclaim. So why do we not do it? Why do we contemplate unshelving parts of ourselves when only we can do it? There are different reasons for all of us. Some think that too much time has passed and it is too late to be who we once were. Some deal with so much regret, guilt, and shame with putting themselves on the shelf in the first place that they become stuck. Others may fear rejection and critique from loved ones for choosing to transform their lives. Whatever the reason, it points to our tendency to value our fears, emotions, and the opinions of others over ourselves.

## Counting Yourself Worthy to Fulfill Purpose

In the struggle with unworthiness, your view of how much you value yourself and your offerings to the world is way below market value. Heaven is our manufacturer and Heaven has placed value on each of us: priceless. That knowledge alone boosts my spirit and puts me in a good mood, but it was not always that way. Unworthiness can be like the bug that flies into your windshield as you are cruising down the highway. If you switch on the wipers without the wiper fluid it can blur your view. When you shelve parts of yourself it blurs how you view yourself. We begin to not view ourselves as worthy of reclaiming. We become stagnant and like a trophy unattended on a shelf we collect dust. We begin to exist instead of living a life of purpose.

It is hard to live a life of purpose when you do not believe you are born with purpose and for a purpose. It is like walking around with a bag of gold, in debt, and being unaware of the purpose of the gold and its value. By Divine design, you have been fearfully and wonderfully made (Psalm 139:14). You were shaped into the person known as, you. To be fearfully made means that when people come in contact with you, they are in awe of you and the Divine presence in your life. To be wonderfully made means to be marked out, distinct, and distinguished by God Himself! Did you know that?! For a good portion of my life, I did not. What I thought was rejection really was my Divine marking that read, "No Trespassing!" The regret, guile, and shame were the result of not maximizing my life's potential and choosing to settle for mediocre instead.

Known or unknown, your purpose is a driving force in your life. When we are living outside of our purposed place in life, we struggle to possess fulfillment and joy. Unworthiness is the thief of fulfillment and joy because it keeps us from pursuing the greatness of purpose in our lives. A lack mentality creates the illusion that we will never be enough to take ownership of our purpose. Our purpose is simply the reason we exist. That is a simple definition of such a great responsibility. When we think about the greatness of God, it can be hard to conceive the thought of God creating us to do a work for His great pleasure. We can even find ourselves displaying a false humility which makes statements like, "I am no one special." Or, "I am not worthy of applause." That mindset and language is contrary to your Divine design. The reality that we are created in the likeness of God means we are special! We may not feel like it all of the time, but that does not make it any less true.

We may not be God, but knowing that His original thought towards us was to create us in His image is mind-blowing! It takes away the excuse of not being worthy of fulfilling purpose. It gives us the responsibility to pursue purpose. Unlearning unworthiness is centered on discarding knowledge proven to be false, binding, or limiting factors that produce unbelief or ignorance about the truth of our worth. The belief that you are not worth applause, success, or love is false. Each one of those blessings is a direct reflection of God in you. You were made to reflect His image in the earth. What an honor to represent Him through our works established through purpose. Life becomes a personal struggle when we are unable to receive our personal assignments with joy and assurance. By getting still and spending time with God through prayer and knowledge of His Word, we are infused with His thoughts towards us.

I tend to look at the Holy Bible as God's love letter to His children. Love letters are filled with emotion where you can vividly see and feel the author's raw feelings towards their object of love. By becoming familiar with our Creator and His love for us, we can easily see and feel His love, longsuffering, grace, and mercy towards us. Our worth in the eyes and mind of such an awesome God will no longer be questioned! Continue to keep His thoughts before you in the good and not so good times no matter what. It will be your strength and anchor when family and friends cannot be found. You will have to walk through some dark seasons of life alone, but God's thoughts towards you are an anchor and strength like no other!

## Unlearning the Effects of Shelving

The process of unshelving to reclaim, restore, and reinstate yourself to wholeness does not have to be scary. Creating this process does not have to be difficult. What unshelving does require are your efforts, commitment and a plan. Action is the greatest enemy of fear and unproductivity. I know this all sounds simple, and in actuality it is, but it does take work. It takes courage to conquer what once held you captive. It takes energy to subdue what once suppressed you. It takes time to heal what once wounded you. During this process, take your time and be patient with yourself. You did not arrive at this place overnight; therefore, you will not arrive at your desired destination overnight. You must learn how to celebrate each step you take towards progress. The key to healing and wholeness is planning your work and working your plan.

After a personal heartbreak, I sought out therapy through a Christian counselor. Although I initially came to her to deal with a broken engagement, we eventually began to set fresh life goals that I wanted to accomplish for personal development. One of my goals was to grow flowers and plant a small garden. We walked through all of the pros and cons of that goal in relation to my schedule and lifestyle. After developing the pro-con list I said, "Man, this is a lot of work!" The counselor's response to me was,

"Well, self-development is work." You can guess what I did after I left; I decided not to grow any flowers or plant a garden. Why? Because I did not believe it was worth all of the work required.

Even though self-development is work, you are worth it. Not only are you worth it, but others who need the lessons you learned to heal are worth it. Your healing is not just for you, it is for others and to God you are all worth it!

## <u>AFFIRMATION</u>

I was born for a purpose.

I live a life of abundance.

I am worth the energy it takes to be whole.

My life is lived with purpose.

**UNlearning Exercises**

1. List the top three areas you have shelved yourself:

   _____

   _____

   _____

2. How has a Lack Mentality manifested in your life?

   _____

   _____

   _____

3. How do you know view yourself in relation to purpose? Do you know your purpose?

   _____

   _____

   _____

4. What steps are you willing to take to progress in your self-development?

   _____

   _____

   _____

# CHAPTER FOUR
## THE POWER TO LOVE

*"Caring for myself is not self-indulgence, it is self-preservation, and that is an act of political warfare."* – Audre Lourdes

Love is an undeniable force. I could take an educated guess and say that we as women have experienced this force in raw form with our first love. First loves, no matter how distant in our past, are unforgettable. We remember what he looked like, how he talked, walked, or even how he smelled. We also can remember how we felt about him and that experience before it ended. The emotions and thoughts that influenced you to do things for the one you loved, you may have not considered doing under normal circumstances. Yes, normal circumstances. Who has not done anything crazy for love? Love, raw love, is not experienced under normal circumstances.

Most of us perceived love to be a radical act of expression that is not liberally given to everyone. Ideally, we would like to think that we have the ability and capacity to love everyone, but the reality is that is a tall order to fill. Instead, we measure who we are able to love and who we are not. I know this sounds harsh, selfish, and insincere, but if we looked at what it means to love, without restraint or judgement, it would be a challenge for most. In God's eternal Word, He demonstrated the highest act of love when He gave His only Son to live a short period of time on earth and gave

His life for those who would accept Him and reject Him (John 3:16). His love for us compelled Him to not only give, but give His best.

Love is rooted in what you are willed to do. Love is not a feeling. Love's companion to your actions is your attitude. Remember that first love? Think about everything you did for them without hesitation. Think about how you felt when you did those things for the one you loved. It was a compelling force to be reckoned with indeed. Now, shift your thoughts to yourself; become the object of your love. Was that hard to do? Did it put a knot in your stomach? If you are anything like me, you learned to love everyone else to the best of your ability, but not yourself. Love is a force and it has power. Learning to love you is one of the best courses you could ever take and lessons to learn.

## Self-love Develops From Learning How to Love

I admit that I can be an idealist from time to time, which makes learning to love all the more difficult for me. Ideals introduce rules and restraints, but love is boundless. Love will reach you at your lowest of lows and highest of highs, but it is not reckless. Learning to love requires you to know the characteristics of love. When you know love's character, you are able to both give and received love from a healthy place. What does love look, feel, or sound like? What is love's swagger? Because a great part of our journey to wholeness and healing involves unlearning old behaviors and thought patterns, let us first learn what love is not.

Abuse of any kind is never acceptable; however, some of us have experienced it. We have experienced physical, sexual, mental, emotional and spiritual abuse.. Sometimes the abuser knew what they were doing, but not why they were doing it. As I have lived and grown in life, I have learned that much of our behavior is learned. Someone, some experience, or environment has taught us how to behave. Some of us have learned what love was through pain and deception. There is no worse pain felt by an invisible wound. Physical wounds being the exception, the average person cannot see our cuts and bruises, but they can be just as damaging. We also learned to love our abuser and believed that they love us. As a result of this, we learned that love came with pain and tolerance.

On my unlearning journey, I traced my first romantic love experience all the way back to middle school. Throughout elementary and middle school I was bullied. I was indeed your typical outcast and had no one to protect me, no one. This is why it was a delightful, but highly questionable, surprise when the most handsome and popular guy in sixth grade wanted me to be his girlfriend. Yes, he was handsome, as handsome as you could be in the sixth grade, but I digress. At first I was hesitant to say yes, but it was the most handsome guy in the sixth grade! How often does that happen to a poor, broken, and bullied girl? For a solid week he walked me to all of my classes, walked me to my bus at dismissal, and gave me his gold rope chain to wear. Back then if a guy gave you his rope chain to wear, he was serious about you, it was a big deal! Then came that Friday afternoon when I was wrapping up my dream come true week as his girlfriend. As he walked me to my bus at dismissal, he told me to give him his necklace back. I naturally asked him, "Why?" He said his chain was required back because he had fulfilled his end of a bet he lost which involved him dating me for a week. I was a bet, a bet. I was devastated. I could not understand why a person would purposely hurt someone who did nothing, but like them.

This experience began the unhealthy mindset of equating love with pain and deception. This cycle would go on for years. My mindset would not allow me to recognize and accept love even when it was real. I would question what was authentic and accept the counterfeit because that is what I learned to do. I would expect the pain and disappointment when it came to love and abuse myself when I would believe it would be any different. Love is not deceptive or has a hidden agenda.

Learning what love is not is less important than learning what love is. I once was told that you know what counterfeit money looks like by studying authentic currency. If you know the characteristics and qualities of what is real, you will be able to spot what is fake a mile away. God has made it easy for us to know what love is and what it is not. 1 Corinthians 13: 4-7 says:

> *"Love suffers and is kind; love does not envy; love does not parade itself, is not puffed up; does not behave rudely, does not seek its own, is not provoked, thinks no evil; does not rejoice in inequity, but rejoices in the truth, hopes all things, endures all things."*

Love is a safe and secure place where we all want to dwell. We must desire to be in a place that welcomes and attracts genuine love. We have an internal and external environment. Unlearning unworthiness teaches us to first create an internal environment where love lives; a place of self-love. Take inventory of your internal environment and be honest about what is there. Your internal inventory includes your emotions, thoughts, and perspective about yourself. This activity may seem a little scary or even trivial, but the rewards are empowerment and self-awareness. When you are aware of any internal issues you are empowered to take control and change them. The power is in your hands. The goal is to create what you do not see, but desire; a healthy environment where self-love exists and thrives.

## Being Okay With Loving Yourself

I read a post somewhere on social media that self-love is a revolutionary act. I could not agree more. What makes it so revolutionary is that it is against most traditional and religious norms which have been taught. Our parents and spiritual leaders have done a great job of teaching us to put others before ourselves and to live a life of humility. These are good principles to live by and are pleasing to God. The challenge is, we are human and some of us tend to live our lives in extremes. Some of us can be extreme givers or takers. Think about how many people you know who depend on your goodness and mercy to always persuade you to give to them whenever they make a request? How many leaders do you know who became discouraged and quit serving because no one considered them and their needs? There is a culture of expectation to give to the point of self-sacrifice. We have become conditioned to expect less from others, but more of ourselves. This expectation can be adopted as a defense mechanism because of the pain of past disappointments. It can also serve as a way to control a disappointing situation. Nonetheless, we must take control of our mindset and change our expectations to achieve both balance and abundance in our lives. We should look to God and His desires for us to internalize an expectation for manifestation. Here is a short list of what we should expect concerning self-love:

1.  We should expect to receive a plan to prosper our lives. – Jeramiah 29:11
2.  We should expect to be healthy in mind, body, and spirit. – 3 John 1:2
3.  We should expect to be whole and possess everything we need through patience on our journey. – James 1:4
4.  We should expect to possess the ability to create wealth in every area of lives. – Deuteronomy 8:18
5.  We should expect God to be magnified and pleased that we are prospering as we serve Him. – Psalms 35:27

Before we were born, God placed loving, positive, blessed expectations before us. If He expects good for us, we should, too. Love from God and ourselves is a Divine expectation. Release yourself from the expectations of others and be at peace with loving yourself.

## Strengthening the Integrity of Your Soul by Guarding Your Heart

The heart is probably the most important part of the human soul. There are other parts of the soul such as the emotions, intellect, and mindset, but the condition of the heart affects them all. The heart is your attitude, moral conscious, and center of your being. If your heart is damaged, not intact, or toxic it affects the integrity of your entire soul. When we think about integrity, we consider a person's morals, ethics, and honesty. If you are an entrepreneur, you measure whether you are going to enter into a partnership or collaboration with another business based upon their character or integrity. This is a good business practice and is wise. This is wise for all types of relationships.

The second most important relationship you will ever invest in (after God) is the one you have with yourself. I have said often that it is unfair to expect people to learn how to deal with you when you are not willing to deal with yourself. Everyone wants the relationship that they choose to be in to be fair. No one enters a fixed fight unless there is a huge payoff. What is the payoff for being in a relationship with someone with unresolved issues? There is no payoff. You are worth the work and energy it takes to be whole. When you put in the work, time, and tears to be the best version of yourself, you will not allow anyone to sneak in and take that progress away. It becomes a sacred process that only you and God know about. Your intimate knowledge of your worth increases your sobriety in guarding your heart. Your heart houses your dreams, hopes, and desires. What you love lives there. When you have created the space for love in your heart towards yourself you have achieved after surviving the negativity, abuse, and projections of other people, you must protect it.

I love ministry, in and outside of the church. Helping, inspiring, and motivating women to be all of what God designed them to be is a joy to me. It is dear to my heart because I have learned how to overcome many of the hurts and challenges that we face as women in this world. We have experienced shame, guilt, disappointment, and heartbreak, yet we still refuse to stay in dark places. We always believe that there are better days ahead and make the choice to be the light to see our way out of the darkness. We are believers of putting in the work. We are worth it. You are worth it. This is why you must place non-negotiable, protective boundaries around your heart space. Here is a brief list of examples of some protective boundaries you should consider when guarding your heart:

1.  Build a strong and consistent prayer life.
    - When you stay connected to God in challenging times, you can always check in and be reminded of who you are from the One who knows you best.

2.  Write down your feelings first before sharing them with others.
    - Sometimes we are not feeling our best and need to vent. Instead of making our friend or spouse the first stop, take the time to pause. Grab your dedicated journal to empty what you are feeling in the moment out of you. One of the most productive and safe ways to do an emotional dump is by journaling. This way, you do not have to fear your feelings in a time of vulnerability being exposed or deal with regret and lack of trust.

3.  Develop a small, but strong, support system invested in your progress.
    - Developing a strong connection with God is essential to securing the integrity of our hearts, but we also need support. God has called us to be inter-dependent, not independent. Have a small circle of people who have tested and proven to be

vested in your best interest. This allows others to bare your pains with strength when you are weak.

Your heart is a valuable and sacred space that must be protected at all costs. It is the unseen part of you that shapes how you view others and yourself. Self-love is essential to a healthy and whole soul. Patience, self-awareness, and support enable you to achieve a healthy balance of loving yourself, first, so that both giving and receiving love is not a struggle.

## <u>Affirmation</u>

I was created by Love.

I was created to love.

I was created to be loved.

I am worthy of love.

## UNlearning Exercises

1.  What was your first experience with love as you know it? Was it healthy or abusive? Why?

     _____

     _____

     _____

2.  Do you have a healthy relationship with yourself? Do you genuinely love yourself? Why or why not?

     _____

     _____

     _____

3.  Have you done a good job protecting your heart in the past? Why or why not?

     _____

     _____

     _____

4.  What safeguards do you/will you have in place to protect your heart?

     _____

     _____

     _____

# CHAPTER FIVE
## HOLY MOMENTS

*"Then shall the dust return to the earth as it was; and the spirit shall return unto God who gave it."* – Ecclesiastes 12:7

Life can take you on many twists and turns. You may not be aware of it, but you are working on getting to a place called "there," or a destined place. Each decision that you make is made with the hope that it is leading you closer to where you desire to be. Frustration can set in when you are unclear on where you are going. How do you know you are on the right track? How do you know you have arrived? These were questions that I had for myself in the summer of 2014. I was struggling internally about a decision I felt led to take that would shift my life in a major way. It felt like a struggle to me because I believed that it would affect one of two areas of my life depending on the choice I made.

As a single woman with no children, I desire to become a wife and a mother. I believe that the roles of being a wife and mother are a part of my destined place. On the other hand, I was feeling the pull to answer the call into ministry by entering into the Minister-In-Training process at my church. I felt that if I said yes to one, it meant no to the other. Being a wife and mother is not just a part of womanhood to me; I believe it is a calling. My goal is to be both a present and dedicated wife to my husband and mother to my children. Both roles take dedication and sacrifice. There is also a high level of sacrifice for the life of a minister. You work for God and He is never off of the clock. I was unclear on how to choose my next step. One day after Sunday church service, I had a brief conversation with one of the ministers at my church and she said something to me that spoke directly to my personal dilemma, *"Once you become settled within, everything around you will become settled."* It was what I call a "holy moment." Immediately, peace filled me internally and I knew what to do; trust God's plan for me and put Him first. I decided to proceed with the Minister-In-Training process and trust that God would give me the desires of my heart. Today, I am a licensed minister and am in earnest expectation of the fulfillment of everything God has put in my heart. I have felt His love for me in a stronger way since that day. I have learned that it is through His love that He reminds us when we are on the right track.

## Love Reminds Us That We Are Enough

People and life circumstances have a way of making you feel that you are not good enough to have great things in life. What is more harmful is when we begin to believe that same lie. We will believe that we are not equipped to live by Divine design. Most of our lives we have learned who we are through different experiences. These experiences either took us from or brought us closer to our original intent. It is easy to allow our circumstances to take us places we did not intend without realizing it. When I was a child I learned how to please people. I was an equal opportunity people pleaser. I was taught that if you did what people wanted you to do and it made them happy, then that was your personal reward. For years, I would run errands, choose sides, and accept unacceptable behavior just to see a person smile. That made me happy. It became my drug, my comfort, and my normal. I developed the belief that I had to do things for people in order to build and maintain relationships. I was taken advantage of time and again. Sometimes I knew I was being abused, and other times I was oblivious to it. Those who used me saw the purity of my heart and perverted it for their pleasure. As a result, I developed vain friendships that made me feel lonely. I recall a childhood experience with two "friends" in my neighborhood where they challenged me to make a tough choice.

They decided one day that I could not be friends with both of them; I had to choose between them. If I said yes to one of them, it was an automatic no to the other; black and white, no shades of gray. What made this situation more interesting is that they were both friends too. This was bullying at its best. Take a moment to search the mind and emotions of a people pleaser. I wanted everyone to be happy. My stomach was in knots for a week because they were very mindful that I needed time to give them my answer. It was brutal! Friday, the day of decision came. That was their favorite time of the week to bring resolution to their torment of me. I made my decision. I chose the friend that I spent most of my time with, knew the longest, and was "kind" to me. I made my choice not realizing that it was a catch 22 from the beginning. No matter who I chose, I was going to lose. As soon as I made my choice, they both laughed, told me that I failed their test, and that neither one of them wanted to be my friend. Devastation and humiliation hit me again.

I entered into a dark place where I believed that the purpose of people in my life was to destroy my spirit. Being a people pleaser is an extreme place to dwell in, but Friendship Gate (that is what I call it) snatched me out of it. It helped me to become aware that I was worth choosing. Before this awareness, I believed that the happiness of others was worth more than the health of my soul. The way that my friends treated me taught me that I was dispensable and worthless, but making that choice shifted my perspective. I learned a new lesson. I unlearned believing that I was not enough. In my new found isolation, I had one of many moments where I would encounter God's love for me. I was in a place where I discovered what I needed. I needed to be reminded of my worth and that God's love is what sustains me, not the approval of others. It would still be years before I put my full trust in God, but whenever I would become disappointed by life or people I would get in a "still" place. A still place is an internal place that is developed through your trust in God and His Divine intention for your life. He reminded me that I was more than enough. This was not always easy to believe because of my emotions. Our negative emotions require us to go in for a deeper revelation of how precious our life is.

## Your Existence is Proof of Your Worth

I love everything about God. One of His character traits that I love most is that He is intentional. God has a purpose and intention for everything He says, does, and creates. Nothing that existed, in existence, or that will exist is without a clear, thought out intention for it. Unworthiness causes us to question the worth of our existence. It is not a bad idea to inquire of God who we are. If you are not curious about something you will not go beyond the surface to discover more. It is like mining your soul for hidden treasure. God tells us:

*"But we have this treasure in earthen vessels, that the excellency of the power may be of God, and not of us."* – 2 Corinthians 4:7

The value of our existence is revealed by knowing the value of our worth. Once we enter into relationship with God, we begin to understand that our existence *is* our worth. We are carriers of God's glory. This is not a common existence. This knowledge shifts the way you see yourself and the way you live. Because you are here, that is all the proof you need that you are worth something. God is intentional! Purpose and intention are what mobilize us to live an abundant and focused life with a worth that is priceless. He desires to use us as vessels of His love and peace. These are gifts He gives each of us access to, but we can only receive them by the knowledge of our worth. Our identity is rooted in God. Our roots are deep and Divine. From the beginning of creation, God declared that who He made was good! A Father's love and affirmation lends credence to our worth being priceless.

## Authentic Relationships Develop Self-Appreciation

It was not until my early thirties that I understood the definition of a true friend. It was then I began to do a lot of introspection and uncover unresolved childhood hurts. My brokenness manifested in dysfunctional behaviors which I normalized. My dysfunction was normal to me. Have you had someone point out something in your character or behavior that was not positive or productive? Was your response, "That's just the way I am. I've always been this way."? I know I have. We all have had our versions and levels of crazy. There were times that I was outright committable! I remember a time during my junior year in high school when my two best friends were preparing for graduation. It was their senior year and all they would talk about was leaving. It made me feel insecure and the fear of abandonment overwhelmed me.

I consider myself to be a functioning introvert and socially awkward. I only had two friends who I trusted; they understood me. I was frightened of the thought of being alone and starting over next year by myself. It had only been my second year living in a new state, new town, and attending a new high school. Being vulnerable and initiating friendships out of my comfort zone frightened me because of my past experiences. One day during lunch, they began to playfully remind me that they were leaving and that next year they would be gone having left me behind. My fear of abandonment screamed out to them, "F--- you!" I told you I was committable. I stormed off and made my way to my afternoon classes, leaving them there frozen in shock of my angry outburst. I am unable to recall if I spoke to either of them for the rest of the day. The next day, I was nervous to face them. I was feeling the guilt of my bad behavior. I had thoughts of them rejecting me, but that never happened. In their way, they asked me what was going on. I explained what I was feeling and why and they forgave me. They never brought it up again.

It was not until I acknowledged and dealt with my brokenness almost twenty years later that I understood the power of authentic relationships and their effect on my self-esteem. These relationships uphold you and support your transformation process. My behavior towards them was unacceptable. I would not have forgiven me as graciously as they did. However, their willingness and ability to love me through my mess helped me to heal. It helped me to learn how to be patient with myself in my growth process. I learned how to acknowledge my dysfunction, unlearn it, and still appreciate who God made me to be.

This enabled me to dig deeper into my relationship with God with confidence. Intimacy with God requires transparency. You can have full assurance that He will not reject you for anything that you share with Him. I used to think that there were some things you could not say to God. I always believed that His holiness should cause us to revere Him and not sin against Him in our speech. As a child in church, I was taught to never question God. I was taught how to have not blind faith, but ignorant faith. There was much I did not know about God because I was taught not to ask Him questions. This behavior goes against the nature of most children, which is to be inquisitive. I remember times I would ask my father my favorite question, "Why?" and his response would be "Don't question me." I was a child being taught not to explore and learn through the process of inquiry.

Warren Berger, author of *A More Beautiful Question*, wrote, "*Anything that forces people to have to think is not an easy sell…*" This knowledge helped me to understand in part why the adults in my life taught me not to ask questions. Most of the time, they did not know the answers to my questions. My questions forced them to dig in and explore for the answer themselves and they simple did not want to do it. My desire was to not be that way; however, I unconsciously adapted this behavior early on in my relationship with God. God knows everything. There is nothing that is hidden from Him. For years I was missing out on depths of intimacy with God because I was taught not to ask Him questions and pour out my heart to Him. Then, one day I thought about it and began to chuckle at the thought of hiding my deepest thoughts from the One who is Omniscient. God already knew my heart and was just waiting for me to freely share it with Him. I chose to stop engaging in struggle through secrecy and embraced transparency in relationships. Being able to let all of my frustrations, desires, and disappointments out in a safe place gives us the ability to release what we were never supposed to carry. Knowing that no matter how ugly, graphic, shameful, or disgusting our thoughts shared may be does not separate you from His love. His love covers everything! To willingly expose your soul to God without fear of betrayal strengthens the integrity of your soul. This type of love compels you into authentic relationship. Things in your heart are revealed that you need to work on while still being able to appreciate our divine essence.

God's will for us is to work our way to His original intent for us. He desires that we ask the questions that only He can answer about ourselves. With Him, we can peel back the layers that cover the beauty of who we are. The closer we get to God the more He shows us who we are. Becoming self-aware can be frustrating, but God's love teaches us to extend patience and grace towards ourselves. It goes beyond our fears and insecurities to empower us to love ourselves.

Our holy moments with God are experiences designed to teach us about the beauty and joy of being who we are by design. These unlearning lessons teach us to love and appreciate who we are from a healthy place. Once we have mastered this lesson, it equips us to love and appreciate others even with their marks of imperfection. It is a gift of security that you cannot purchase from ADT Home Security. This love allows for liberation of your soul to heal itself. God accepts you and He desires that you accept yourself.

## <u>AFFIRMATION</u>

I was originally created and declared as good.

I love who I am and accept all of me.

I am more than my mistakes.

My existence is my worth.

## UNlearning Exercises

1. What do you not like about yourself? Why?

   _____

   _____

   _____

2. What have you done in the past that you are unable to forgive yourself for?

   _____

   _____

   _____

3. List the relationships that support your transformation of progress.

   _____

   _____

   _____

4. Are you being transparent with God about what is in your heart? Why or why not?

   _____

   _____

   _____

# CHAPTER SIX
## FACE-TO-FACE

*"You never find yourself until you face the truth."* – Pearl Bailey

Childhood can be tough. It can be brutal because children lack emotional maturity and are most honest in those formative years. For these reasons, childhood has been the least favorite years of my life, but the most educational. It was in my childhood that I learned to confront my fears. I was not always successful, but I learned the importance of confrontation. As I have mentioned before, I was bullied as a child. Bullying has a way of placing you in an invisible prison that you are always plotting to escape. From my experience with bullying, I understand why a child would choose the way of escape through suicide. He or She just wants the suffering to stop. I also had a moment when I wanted resolution.

One day in middle school on a bus ride home, I had an eerie feeling; a feeling I knew all too well. The feeling of knowing you are about to have a bullying experience. We were coming to the stop right before my bus stop when a boy from my neighborhood began to start an argument with me. His behavior confirmed the feeling I had. I tried to reason with him by telling him that I did not want any trouble, but he was relentless. It was as if he was under a demonic influence that drove him to declare that he was going to "fight me like a man." As we were approaching my stop, I franticly was thinking of the quickest way to get off of the bus and run home. Needless to say, my plan did not work as he was quicker and stronger than me. He did just what he said he would; fought me like a man. In my futile attempts to protect myself, I fought back thinking, "Why isn't anyone helping me?" Then suddenly, relief came in the form of an older woman in the neighborhood who pulled him off of me. The beating was over. I ran home being thankful to have escaped with only a swollen face, busted lip, and a sore body. Mentally and emotionally, I was fragmented, but I left learning my first lesson in the important life principle of confrontation.

**Confrontation Takes the Fear Out of Self-Discovery**

I remember how much I pleaded with the boy from my neighborhood that day. I just wanted him to leave me alone. I attempted to avoid conflict to no avail, but it taught me what it looked and felt like to engage in confrontation. Did I have to deal with the verbal, emotional, and physical assault that I suffered? No. However, it was necessary for me to learn the entire process of facing, in defiance, anything that threatens my well-being. The average person does not enjoy confrontation. It is an emotional process that can get the best of you if you allow it. Fear enters in to overtake the process, but what is fear really? God says to us:

*"God has not given us a spirit of fear, but of power, love, and a sound (self-discipline) mind."* – 2 Timothy 1:7

Fear is anything that robs you of your power, love, and self-discipline whenever you are challenged to grow.

1.  **Fear is a thief of your personal power.**
    We were all born with the ability to accomplish whatever God puts in our hands. There are times when we come to the end of our own strength and must rely on God's strength alone. When fear is in control, you feel powerless and choose the option of doing nothing by default. You become paralyzed by

the thought of doing anything. There were times when I would convince myself to wait for things to change. Day after day, I held on to the hope that the bullies in my life would either leave me alone or realize they were wrong. That day never came. Things only changed when I changed. When I stopped running from and pleading with the thing I feared the most and confronted it is when changed occurred.

2.  **Fear is the thief of love.**
    Love is a powerful force that keeps you in perfect peace even in the most challenging times. When we extend love to ourselves to heal from past hurts, we enable ourselves to move forward with no root of bitterness in our hearts. God says:

    *"There is no fear in love. But perfect love casts out fear, because fear involves torment."* – 1 John 4:18

    Pure love drives fear away in confrontation and frees us to deal with what is bullying us. Love enables you to be free to be your best self.

3.  **Fear is the thief of self-discipline.**
    Our emotions can be a blessing or a curse. When faced with the challenge of confrontation. When we are not in control of our emotions we are inclined to make emotional decisions based out of fear. Some of the fear-based decisions we make can look like lying, shutting people out emotionally, or quitting a job abruptly. A disciplined mind will not allow you to give in to your soul's emotional requests. Fear is always baiting you to jump off of a cliff or burn a bridge when the soul is wounded. The power of discipline always considers the need for healing, not the desire for revenge.

When overcoming the fear of healing from past hurts, we must keep in mind that many of the experiences were out of our control.

The child within you can struggle with baring the responsibility of what happened, but the adult who is now leading knows better. You have wisdom, understanding, and compassion. As an adult, I now see the bullying experiences as lessons on confrontation. The more I confronted the bullies, the less afraid of them I became; even if the outcome was not favorable. The more I confronted the bullies, the more I discovered who I was and what I was made of inside.

Bullies come in different forms and intensities. For some, it may be fear of darkness and things that go bump in the night. For others, the bully can be the fear of being alone. For me, the bully was the fear of confrontation. Confrontation for many is sickening. I understand how your body can physically respond that way. There are so many variables in a confrontation and if it is not done with wisdom, it can go wrong quickly. Even with the various things that can happen, the one thing that is constant is the opportunity for self-reflection. Facing yourself is challenging. Naturally, we are inclined to think the best of ourselves at all times. We can be aware of negative behaviors we are engaging in, but will minimize its effects. We do this to buffer the blow this type of awareness delivers to our ego. We fight or flight as a response to the confrontation. According to Google.com, the Fight or Flight Response is:

*The instinctive physiological response to a threatening situation, which readies one either to resist forcibly or to run away.*

Confrontation is not always desirable so we must choose to fight our way through it. When you choose to confront an issue/person that is bullying you, you are choosing to save yourself. You choose to become your own hero. When you choose to fight, you step into your courage. It may not look good, it may not feel good, but you discover the invitation to be better. Growth requires work.

## Focus on the Promise, Not the Work

Focus is a powerful force. It can lead you into a ditch or to a pot of gold at the end of a rainbow. What is given the most attention is what is nurtured to grow, good or bad. When we engage in confrontation for self-development the focus can be put more on the work instead of the promise. I do not subscribe to the school of thought that work can be fun if you find your passion in it. I understand that work is necessary for progress. Some of the most important work that we do is tedious, that is why some of us avoid it. For progress' sake, I had to shift my focus. I decided to focus on what I was gaining instead of what I had to do to obtain it. This did not eliminate thoughtful actions that were necessary to take, but it was no longer a focal point of my process. The promise of the process became the object of my desire.

This principle is used by companies in their marketing and sales efforts. Every successful company knows what you need, but they market what you want. Nike knows that you need a quality pair of athletic sneakers, but they market to you images of being the best in the persons Michael Jordan and LeBron James. Unless you understand how marketing a product or service works, you can easy miss this principle. I made a decision to shift how I marketed the work of my progress to the actual promise of my process. In business, this can be referred to as the brand promise.

For all intents and purposes, I will call this your Personal Brand Promise (PBP). With the help of smithconsultancy.com, PBP is defined as:

"One that connects your purpose, your positioning, your actions, and your desired life experience."

1.  Purpose – you are here for a reason and your existence is important to God's plan. Your PBP should connect to your

personal purpose. If it does not serve your purpose, it should not be included in your PBP.

2.  Positioning – where you are in life should be reflected in your PBP. Your position physically, emotionally, spiritually, mentally, financially, and socially affects your brand promise. Take inventory of each area and if it does not align with the promise you are making to yourself, create a plan to move and execute it!

3.  Actions – what you do to obtain your promise of progress should be intentional and purposeful. Actions are a result of your will. Get clear on your true intent and take the actions to align with it.

4.  Designed Life Experience – what do you want? It is a simple question that can be challenging to answer. It is hard to answer because we do not know or have taken the time to explore what we really want, but once we do we become accountable to it. Be honest with yourself about what you want and commit to the experience.

Once you take an assessment of developing your Personal Brand Promise for yourself, your focus on intentional confrontation will give you comfort instead of dread.

## Confrontation Brings Comfort and Hope

Coming face to face with what is keeping you stagnant is always an invitation to become your best self. Being stuck in neutral is an act of futility. Not making a decision is a decision. Deciding not to confront an obstacle is deciding to not cross the bridge for you to arrive at your destined place. I hate bridges with a passion. If I am the passenger in a car and we must cross a bridge, I will follow my protocol of bracing myself and closing my eyes until we have made it safely to the other side. I know we have made it to the other side because of the change in the sound of the car from the bridge to the highway, along with how the ride in the car feels. If I am driving the car, for obvious reasons I am unable to close my eyes, but I will brace myself on the steering wheel and hold my breath. I do not look to the left or to the right, only straight forward. It does not matter how beautiful the scenery is going across the bridge, I choose to forfeit that experience of beauty and deal with the discomfort of crossing the bridge. I let go of becoming awe struck with what I see and focus only on getting to the other side where comfort is waiting for me.

This is what gives me hope in spite of what I feel; getting to the other side. When I am the passenger, I am at the mercy of the driver's speed. When I am the driver, I control the speed that it takes to cross the bridge. I will admit that I increase my speed when crossing over a bridge! I also exercise wisdom because my intent is not to cause an accident on the way to my goal. These are things to be mindful of when you are facing your bully or even yourself. On our way to the land of comfort and hope, we should be intentional about accomplishing our goals in peace.

Confrontation is the bridge we use to cross over to our goals, not to burn when we have achieved them. It is our hope that we will cross the bridge only once, but it is an expectation that it will be used by others who follow after you. Unlearning behaviors and mindsets that cause us to not experience a life of liberty and abundance is not only for us, but for those we are chosen to teach. Once we learn, we teach. Once we teach, we heal. Once we heal, we deliver. Life continues to teach us the importance of personal wholeness for the purpose of collective wholeness.

On your unlearning journey you will face fear, frustration, and discomfort but it should not cause you to lose your focus for progress. Your relationship with God will guide you to where He destines for you to be. Emotions will arise and possibly create obstacles on your path but avoid discarding them. Instead allow your emotions to be guideposts. Your emotions of discomfort help to guide you to where your pain points are located in the soul. This is important for total healing. Feeling uneasy on your journey through life is actually a good thing to experience. It is ok, to not feel ok. Pull into a rest area to explore those feelings so that you can be emotionally healthy for a successful journey.

## <u>AFFIRMATION</u>

I hold the keys to my liberation.

I confront what confines me.

I will pursue my comfort and hope.

I will possess the promise of my purpose.

**UNlearning Exercises**

1. Do you have anyone or anything that bullies you? If so, what/who are they?

   _____

   _____

   _____

2. Are you challenged with confronting your bullies? If yes, why?

   _____

   _____

   _____

3. Based off of the description in this chapter, write out your Personal Branding Promise (PBP).

   _____

   _____

   _____

4. What is the bridge that you are/have crossed that you must help others cross?

   _____

   _____

   _____

# CHAPTER SEVEN
## MASTER THE TEACHER

*"Be like water making its way through cracks. Do not be assertive, but adjust to the object, and you shall find a way around or through it. If nothing within you stays rigid, outward things will disclose themselves...Be water, my friend"*
– Bruce Lee

Math is one of my favorite subjects. I would love to tell you that as an engineer, I was some type of prodigy who spent her spare time as a child working on theoretical calculus problems, but that was not the case. Mathematics was, and can still be, a challenging subject for me. Yet, I still love it! No, I am not a glutton for punishment, but I am a sucker for anything that is not easy. During my sophomore year in high school, I took Algebra II with my favorite teacher that we called Dr. Sethu. Dr. Sethu is a short, quirky, mathematical genius from India. I always wondered how a man such as this wound up teaching math in the poor, rural, predominately African American town of Kingstree, SC. I have attributed his arrival and residency there as me and countless others being the beneficiaries of divine providence. I am so thankful he was led there nonetheless because his teaching gift kept giving of itself to me beyond high school graduation.

As a child, and into adulthood, I was an overachiever. I always set goals to earn perfect scores on my math and science tests. Was that realistic? Maybe, maybe not, but it was always my goal. Once after receiving our scores back from an Algebra II test, I expected to have earned a perfect score. Cue the violins, I earned a 92. After class, I went to Dr. Sethu to discuss my errors that prevented me from earning a 100 and he said something that I would never forget. He explained to me that my score could have been lower, but I showed my math so that he could see where I went wrong. I learned the importance of showing my math, showing all of my work, so that I could track any mistakes I may have made.

Often times, we are unable to create a clear path to a necessary solution in our lives because we have arrived at places based off of taking shortcuts. Shortcuts are not a bad thing to utilize, but if you ever get lost on a back road, it can put you in a bind. Naturally, we love shortcuts. Anything that you use to shorten the learning curve is a plus. However, there is always something missed when a shortcut is taken. You may miss the beauty of the scenic route and the awe of time in peace and solitude on your quest to arrive at your destination in accelerated time. In life, when we take shortcuts to our destined place, we can miss lessons, principles, and holy moments because of impatience and immaturity. In our rush to get to the place called *there*, there are pieces of ourselves we fail to discover and filter through in order to arrive as our best selves. We fail to do the work. We fail to show our work. We are unable to track where we made a wrong turn because we did not do the math. Doing the math in our lives is important because math can be trusted. Numbers do not lie and they have no agenda. Looking at the math of your life is like looking at the truth of your life.

Teachers have a responsibility to teach what they have learned to their assigned students. My 7th grade math teacher would always tell us that if we were unable to teach someone how to successfully work through a math problem it was because we did not understand it ourselves. How well do you understand your own problems? Have you found the solution(s) to the problem(s)? If so, have you done the math and have the work to prove it? The math is where the details are, and those details contain the keys to your own deliverance. One detail that I discovered through my problem-solving process was that my process was unique to me. Although my issues were not unique, my process to my solution was. Standards that are set by people are good to have as a guide, but they are not exact. Standards are a great place to start, but when it comes to your life's process there should be room to consider you in it. Consideration of your family background, temperament, life experiences, and your purpose just to name a few, should be taken.

A great part of what it takes to mastering the teacher is by becoming self-aware. It is challenging to increase in personal development if you do not know yourself. It is important in simple things such as likes and dislikes, to more complex things such as triggers and temperament. I believe this aspect of self-mastery, mastering the teacher, is necessary because it enables you to honor your purpose and calling. If you are unable to first become knowledgeable of yourself, it is hard to know what your service to others looks like. The concept that we are all teachers may be hard to grasp, but it is impossible to escape. You are a teacher and you have a subject specialty.

In part, an effective teacher is successful in separating their God-given temperament from personality adaptations. Because life can be eventful, traumatic, joyous, and disappointing all at the same time, we create ways to adapt to it all. We adapt to environments as they change and challenge who we are, or cause our true selves to rise up. In the former case, we are susceptible to developing personality traits that are harmful to our purposeful temperament. An example of this could be the young lady who is negatively outspoken, but was created to be an advocate or spokesperson for a group of people who do not have the strength or courage to speak up for themselves. One is ineffective and the other is effective. This distinction can only be made clear when we step out of fear and into courage. It takes courage to see, acknowledge, and confront the unproductive areas of our lives. It does not feel good to know about the parts of ourselves that are more self-serving than a service to others. It can cause you to feel a sense of shame to know that a personality trait you have guarded for years was never a part of your original intent, but a choice. You can make a new choice to grow into who was always there. It only takes making a decision to choose you.

**You Must Position Yourself to Win So Others Can Win.**

Positioning yourself to be the best you as possible is essential for personal development and purpose fulfillment. Positioning takes *practice*, *intention*, and *consistency*. Being positioned for success holistically is always the goal, but these are a few areas to focus on that are foundational for everyone. As you continue to dig deep and become aware of the areas of focus for your journey, add them to your process and list:

1. Spiritual Positioning
   For you to be firmly established in your worth, you must be positioned in a relationship with God through Jesus Christ. This is the most important position to take as it shapes the path you choose to take in life. Your Divine intent is in your spiritual positioning.

   Practice: Every day, set aside time to build your spiritual position through prayer, study of His Word, application of His Word, and meditation on His Word. Even a board certified doctor is practicing medicine in an effort to master their position, so be not concerned with perfection. You are being perfected in your practice.

   Intention: Develop the attitude of relationship building with God. Just as a man pursues a woman that he desires to marry her, you must be intentional about pursuing God. This can be done through purchasing books, watching videos, and having iron-sharpening conversations for the sole purpose of spiritual edification.

   Consistency: Secure your spiritual space so that hindrances and distractions are eliminated to keep you consistent. This may look like distancing yourself from people who are offended by your commit to Christ and surrounding yourself with those who are not. Do what you need to set yourself up for success, consistently.

2. Mental Positioning

How you think influences what your think about. This in part also affects your emotions. Your mind can take you to places you never desired to go. Proverbs 23:7 says, *"For as he thinks in his heart, so is he."* We think, or not think, our way through life. What we think about ourselves determines the actions we do or neglect to take to position ourselves for a productive life. When you know the truth of who you are, you are able to meditate, then act on what you believe your position in life should be.

> Practice: Every day, when a thought contrary to what you know to be true comes to mind, practice thinking about the truth. You can take it step further and write out the truth and post it throughout your home and work space. Also, practice rehearsing the truth out loud. *"Faith comes by hearing, and hearing by the Word of God."* – Romans 10:17.

> Intention: Become relentless in thinking about anything that is an enemy to your truth. This can be done through immediately confronting the thought as soon as it comes to mind. Or, you can share your goals with your support system of family and friends who can help hold you accountable of your thoughts through the words that you speak.

> Consistency: Bring your thoughts into harmony by first agreeing with what God has said about them. He has informed us that *"For my thoughts are not your thoughts, neither are your ways my ways, saith the Lord. For as the heavens are higher than the earth, so are my ways higher than your ways, and my thoughts than*

*your thoughts.*" – Isaiah 55:8-9. Rest in knowing that
His thoughts are consistently on a higher plane
than yours, but be aware that we must work at
elevating mentally to agree with Heaven.

3. Physical Positioning
Environment is everything. Being in the right environment
for any living thing or being could mean the difference
between life and death. I have an African violet plant that I
have had for almost 3 years. I must admit that I am rather
impressed with myself that it is still alive. Since I did not
know much about the plant when I first received it, I did a
little research on it. I learned that it thrives best indoors
and with plenty of sunlight. This meant that I needed to
place it on a window ceil inside of my home that receives
lots of sunlight. I also learned that it is best to not allow
the leaves to get wet when watering it, so I brought a
planter that I could water from the bottom, therefore,
allowing only the roots and soil to come in contact with
the water. As the plant grew and I needed to repot the
plant with soil specifically for African violets. Yes, just as
meticulous as I have to be with a common household
plant, you must be with your physical positioning.

> Practice: Every day, check in with yourself about
> how you feel in your environment. Is it conducive
> for your growth as a person? If not, remove
> yourself from or remove things out of your
> environment. This may mean changing your eating
> habits that effect your physical being, moving to a
> new neighborhood or seeking employment with a
> business where you can bloom. Taking inventory
> of your physical positioning is not an option, it is a
> necessity.

> Intention: Setting goals for your physical
> positioning speaks to your intent. You will act on

what you believe and have set your heart to do. When you set goals for yourself physically, you are placing your intentions on a course to an expected end. WRITE THEM OUT. It may seem elementary, but it is essential to your success.

Consistency: With anything practical, success is accomplished with accountability. Seek out people who are successful in the areas of life you are working on and follow them. This may require a financial investment, but it will certainly require an investment of time and action. Sharing your written or verbal goals with them puts you in a place where you are not only accountable to yourself, but someone else. It is easy to give yourself a pass when you fall short, but someone else who is also invested in your success will not.

To thrive as the teacher you are, you must set up your life's classroom with intention. You must know what you need to teach your life's lessons successfully. Where you are, who is around you, who is listening to you, and who you are listing to are all important.

We are all designed to prosper. Spiritually, God designed us to seek out and desire a connection with the Source of our spiritual being. He has spoken that everyone who hungers and thirsts for a progressive and intimate relationship with Him would have their desire filled (Matthew 5:6). Everyone, no matter which path they choose, ultimately is desiring to grow spiritually. By entering into relationship with God through Jesus Christ, we plug in and connect to the path of spiritual prosperity. By Divine design we are also inclined to grow mentally. This is why we go to school, why libraries are built, and why there are bookstores around the world. With increased knowledge, we increase in awareness of ourselves and the world around us. Physically, it is no secret that we are designed to prosper. We come into the world as a baby, and by the grace of God we leave the world as an elder. The best teachers are those who are clear that their life is an evolution into who God purposed them to be. They are intentional in living a life that leads them in the direction of that perfected place.

## Self-Mastery Requires You to Empty Yourself.

When I was in college one of the several classes I needed extra help in was Thermodynamics. My professor, Dr. Joseph, was a cute version of Colonel Sanders, but with modern day clothing. I would go to his office often to gain more clarity on the lessons so I could complete the class successfully. I loved him as a teacher because he was so humble and touchable which was a complete contrast to many of my other mechanical engineering professors. However, there was one thing about my visits with him that would leave me frustrated each time I left his office. Every question that I asked him, he would never give or offer me the answer. He would always answer me with a question to assist me in reaching the solution myself. At the time, it would frustrate me, but as I matured I began to understand his purpose behind this teaching technique.

One of the reasons he would not outright give me the answer to a question I asked was because it would hinder me from doing my due diligence to dig deeper and discover the answer for myself. If he would have just given me the answer, it would have conditioned me to rely on him as the source of my answers rather than a resource. The other, and most powerful, realization that I came to was that his questions to me were his way of teaching me that the answers were always within me. No matter what question I had for him, he taught me that I possessed the answer.

Does this mean that we possess the answer to every question we will ever have? No, not at all. What Dr. Joseph taught me was the importance of pulling out what I thought I did not have to give. By him asking me the right questions, he caused me to shift my perspective and develop my way to the solution. The best teachers are intentional about pouring out all that they know to help others. There is nothing selfish about how they teach. It gives them great joy and energy to pour out from their well of knowledge. Self-mastery requires you to acknowledge your responsibility to share what you have learned with others. This helps to ensure there is perpetual healing and prospering of those we are assigned to serve. Maya Angelou said best, *"When you learn, teach, when you get, give."* This is how we learn to master the teacher.

We are constantly learning lessons. In this book, the lesson is focused on unlearning unworthiness. Part of the lesson is to unlearn the thought that we do not have anything to teach or give. You are worthy and have something to give as a teacher. All of the trauma and trials that you have come out on the other side of in one piece is your lesson plan. Will old thoughts and habits try to hinder you from moving forward? Yes, but now you are different. You no longer live for perfection, but progression. Unlearning anything is a process. Unlearning unworthiness is a process where you steadily are learning something new that you must teach, then do it all over again. It does not stop, and you should not either. Mastery takes time and patience. Take the time that you need to heal and give yourself grace during the process. Why? Because you are worth it!

## <u>Affirmation</u>

I am committed to my process of healing.

I am a student and a teacher of my life lessons.

When I learn, I teach, and repeat.

I am a student and a teacher of unlearning unworthiness.

**UNlearning Exercises**

1. What is your God-given temperament vs. your personality traits?

_____

_____

_____

2. What are your goals for positioning yourself to win?

_____

_____

_____

3. What is your life's lesson that you must teach? Why?

_____

_____

_____

4. What are you willing to do to position you to be the best student and teacher of your lifeclass?

_____

_____

_____

# AFTERWORD

As you reflect on the powerful literally gift that Lorea has provided for all of us, I encourage you to pause. What rises to the very top of your spirit and mind? What quote or sentence has left a permanent imprint on your heart? I ask because knowing Lorea very well, I know that her intent is always to love, educate and inspire. As a woman of God and light, she has always served as a voice and vessel for others. Our journeys came together in during a time that we both could have learned from the very book you are holding in your hands.

The purpose of an Afterword is to typically describe how a work of art came about. This book is a manifestation, based on my observation, of Lorea's obedience. As an entrepreneur, daughter, and friend, I have witnessed her sacrifice greatly for others. Our relationship began several years ago, with Lorea as a consulting client and retail startup. That relationship authentically evolved into a bit of personal development support and eventually a friendship.

During the relationship, we spoke openly about life, business, love, family and the importance of healing. It was undeniable that this would be our greatest bond. Although business united us, our love for people, service, and the inner journey of healing became the unifier that has carried us into the current chapter.

It is an honor to be a part of this project because it is very rare that we witness a person, commit to navigating the muddy waters, make mistakes, get hurt, and choose to rise and share. It is easy for many to rise out of the need for sheer survival, but it is completely different to rise and want to reach back and share what we have learned. This is critical, because it is through the sharing and the authentic exchange of experiences that we begin to awaken other areas of ourselves.

The most beautiful memory that I have with Lorea as it relates to this wonderful work of art, is the evolution of her relationship with her father. There was a time when it was filled with much pain and walking on egg shells. After her father became ill, Lorea chose to sacrifice many dreams and entrepreneur projects to be present for him. She became a care taker and began to truly embrace whatever it was that God had for both. I recall tough conversations, emotional waves, frustration, truth, joy and love. Sometimes, the love we desire most is just a conversation away. I love how Lorea explains the importance of self-love and making room to receive healthy love in chapter four.

The relationship with her father is the perfect example of when I began to witness Lorea welcome and embrace a new level of love. Just prior to her father passing away, I recall her being in such a peaceful place with their relationship. I knew in my heart that God had done something powerful with them. I knew it would change her life forever. Little did either of us know that it would be passed on to you and the rest of the world.

I have found in my own journey that we never know what we are called to face head on. What I do believe is that it is always for someone besides us. As we become better people, the world around us does as well.

I want to congratulate you for caring enough to invest in a tool that has hopefully inspired you to truly love yourself where you are and know that you are worthy of your heart's desires. I also congratulate Lorea Sample, for being an obedient vessel and servant who continues to be a light in the world and in the lives of others including my own. God bless.

Love,

Tierra Destiny Reid
Consultant, Author, Entrepreneur
Author of *The Power of Peace in a Pause* ©2014

# ABOUT THE AUTHOR

Speaker | Engineer | Entrepreneur | Author

Lorea M. Sample is a native of South Carolina, grew up in Philadelphia and now resides in Columbia, SC. As a 2001 graduate of Clemson University, she earned my Bachelor of Science Degree in Mechanical Engineering Clemson University in Clemson, SC and has enjoyed a 10+ year career as an Environmental Engineer.

She also is a purpose-driven entrepreneur who coaches women to build profitable, faith-centered lives and businesses through her women empowerment brand, Faith Builder.

For speaker inquiries, please visit loreasample.com or contact her at bookings@loreasample.com.

www.ingramcontent.com/pod-product-compliance
Lightning Source LLC
LaVergne TN
LVHW052036080426
835513LV00018B/2342